Python Programming for Beginners

The Most Comprehensive Programming Guide to Become a Python Expert from Scratch in No Time.
Includes Hands-On Exercises

Cory Reed

ISBN: 979-8354101856
10 9 8 7 6 5 4 3 2 1

< GET YOUR BONUS NOW! >

To walk you through the journey of learning Python programming, in collaboration with Jason Welt and Sarah Allen, I have created two guides on time management and productivity strategies that will help you get the most out of this book.!

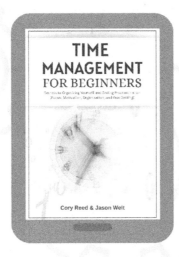

To download your bonuses scan the following QR code

or go to

https://books-bonuses.com/cory-reed-bonuses

All the bonuses are completely FREE and you won't have to leave any personal details except your name and email address.

Table of Contents

Chapter 1: Introduction to Python

What is Python?

Python is a high-level, general-purpose programming language that emphasizes code readability. Python is used in many domains and can be applied in various ways depending on your specific needs. Some of the most shared uses are web development, data science, machine learning and artificial intelligence (AI), system administration, and so much more. Guido van Rossum first released the language in 1991.

The name "Python" was chosen to reference simplicity, clear syntax and readability. Python is also well-suited to developing dynamic web applications because it is a high-level language emphasizing code readability over low-level memory management. Put another way, it's easy to tell what your code does without caring about how it does it.

One of Python's most critical features is its emphasis on readability. With Python, you can easily read and understand code written by other people (or yourself if you've forgotten how it works). The language syntax allows developers to express their ideas in fewer lines, making the code easier to maintain and support rapid prototyping.

Python was designed with a bias towards readability and a very clean syntax. This makes it easier to maintain and support. Python is used by some of the world's most influential companies, including Google, NASA and Reddit. Many large web service providers like YouTube, Instagram and Pinterest also use Python on their back-end to power their services.

Python's popularity is reinforced by the fact that it has an extensive online community. The language has many official documentation channels, including tutorials, videos, and books that are easy to find online. GitHub also lists over 150,000 projects that are all written in or include Python.

How can you benefit from this book?

Python programming looks easy to implement, but it isn't. It would help if you were thorough about several foundational topics that Python comes with and should be aware of the techniques that will let you utilize these foundations to solve problems. This book provides you with theoretical knowledge that can help you understand the foundations and help you have practical experience with the programming language you are trying to use.

To get the most out of this book, we recommend cognitive learning techniques to enhance your experience with this material.

Use mind maps to map different concepts and quickly implement them in your projects. Mind maps are cognitive learning tools that use visual excellence to easily remember a lot of data with just a detailed diagram.

Use cognitive memory techniques such as Memory Palace to remember the data with a sense. There is a difference between mugging up and storing the required information in your brain using cognitive techniques.

Use the passive recall technique to quickly revise all the topics you have learned in this book. Passive recall can help you to strengthen your programming foundations.

Use the Feynman technique and explain all basic programming concepts you have learned in this book to someone unaware of the subject. You are strong with the core foundations if you can demonstrate a concept in simple words.

Don't just use the code given in the book. Reimplement your code using similar strategies. The simple copy and paste technique will not help you create your code.

Python as a programming language expects you to be as innovative as possible. Treat programming with Python as a puzzle, and you will soon find ways to trick your brain into creating complex code logic for real-world problems. This book helps you to become as effective as possible with Python programming. We are excited to start the journey with you. Are you ready?

Chapter 2: Getting Started with Python

History of Python

The creator of Python, Guido van Rossum, created Python as a casual project during a Christmas holiday. He used his experience while working with the ABC programming language to create an interpreted programming language that is intuitive and easier for programmers to work with. With his expertise in Unix development, he first used Python to impress hackers in an online community.

However, due to his response from his fellow programmers, he started to polish it for several months to create a programming language that was concise, simple, and fast. For his contributions to the Python project, Guido van Rossum has been named the benevolent dictator of the Python community. This high award can be bestowed upon open-source developers.

Right from its release, Python has consistently been one of the top 10 popular programming languages according to TIOBE rankings. Python's minimalistic approach to solving problems has helped it defeat other programming languages, such as Pearl, to become one of the more approachable programming languages for beginners.

Python uses the philosophy of "There is only one way to solve a problem," which contradicts the philosophy of programming languages such as Pearl, which supports "There are different ways to solve a problem." Python gave much-needed discipline to the programming community and made software development rise exponentially.

To understand how impactful Python was to programmers worldwide, look at the below-mentioned Applications of Python.

Applications of Python

Python marked its impact in different domains of modern science & technology.

1. Web Domain

Python as a programming language has made most of its initial impact on web technology. While Java was ruling the webspace, Python was not so popular. With time, several third-party frameworks such as Django and Tornado have helped Python to become popular with web developers.

Fast forward two decades, Python is now one of the most popular scripting languages for websites, standing only next to Javascript. Several multinational companies such as Google, Facebook, and Netflix use Python in their software implementations. Django, a famous web framework, can help programmers to write backend code for several APIs.

Python is also popular with automation, so bots such as Pinflux are often developed using it.

2. Scientific Computing Domain

Python is popular with the scientific community due to its open-source nature. Software such as Numpy and Scipy helps computer scientists to conduct computational experiments with less code. As Python also works better with mathematical calculations and software, there is no other alternative for Scientists other than Python these days.

3. Machine Learning and Artificial Intelligence

Both machine learning and Artificial intelligence are right now two combined technologies that offer more jobs to developers. Python has a lot of third-party libraries, such as Tensorflow, that is entirely focused on Machine learning algorithms implementation.

Python also has excellent adaptability to Deep learning and Natural language processing technologies, making it one of the core contenders for becoming a better language for developing Artificial intelligence-related technology.

4. Linux and Database Management

With growing companies worldwide, there is a lot of demand for Develop engineers who can effectively manage databases and internal systems. While Develop engineers need to have enough knowledge about different operating systems such as Linux, they also need to have enough knowledge about Python to automate other procedures that are essential for checking the performance of methods on an internal network.

Different Versions of Python

Python is a general-purpose, high-level programming language. Guido Van Rossum developed it in the late 1980s and early 1990s. Python is a dynamic, interpreted programming language that allows code to be executed without being compiled into machine-readable instructions.

The most popular versions of Python are 2.x and 3.x, but many professionals still use Python 2 because it's less buggy than its successor (as well as has more libraries). However, Python 2.x is no longer being maintained so it won't be updated with new features. Python 3.x is the best version to learn and use because it has the most developers' support and many new features (it's also backwards-compatible with Python 2.x).

Python version summary:

Python 2.x: This version is still widely used but will not be updated with new features because its creator (Guido Van Rossum) has abandoned it in favor of Python 3.x.

Python 3.x: This is the best version because it has many new features and is less buggy than Python 2.x.

Python 2.7: This version is more popular than Python 3, but it's still highly recommended to learn and use Python 3 instead. It's also the default version for Windows, Linux, OS X, and UNIX systems; however, this rule has some exceptions (Microsoft Windows has not officially supported any version since Windows 10).

Python 3.6: This version is most prevalent in academia but seems to have a smaller userbase than Python 2.x, especially in enterprise environments (it also has less support for Python 2).

Python 3.5: A newer version of Python with many new features and bug fixes; it's the most popular version nowadays. You can get more information about the various versions of Python here.

Python 3.4: This version is still the alternative to Python 3.5 because Python 2.x is no longer supported.

Python 3.3: This was the last feature-complete version before Python 3 started to make significant changes; most were backwards incompatible with previous versions, and some have been removed (such as the set module).

Python 2.7: This is the last version of Python that's still compatible with Python 3.x; however, it's not as popular as Python 3.x and has less support in enterprise environments. This version targets new developers because it's the default version in Cydia Impactor, an app that helps you install jailbroken iOS applications on your iPhone or iPad (and currently only supports Windows and Linux).

What Are the Benefits?

The benefits of Python include easy and interactive learning, readability, rapid development, and prototyping. This language supports modular programming, information hiding, object-oriented programming, dynamic typing, and automatic memory management. There are no limits on the expressiveness or complexity of your code. Python can serve as a scripting language for web applications; it has also been used for commercial products, web services, and to create desktop applications.

Installing Python

Since we have learned a little more about Python, it's time to look at some of the steps involved in installing Python on your computer. You want to ensure that you can adequately navigate and install this program and that the correct version is installed on your computer at the appropriate time. This will make writing some of the necessary code easier without encountering too many roadblocks.

Install the interpreter

Before we can begin writing our first Python program, we must first download the Python interpreter appropriate for our computers. Python 3 will be used in this book because, as the official Python website stated, "Python 2.x is legacy; Python 3.x is the language's present and future." Additionally, "Python 3 eliminates numerous quirks that can unnecessarily confuse inexperienced programmers."

However, it is worth noting that Python 2 is still quite popular. Python 2 and 3 are approximately 90% identical. Thus, if you learn Python 3, you will almost certainly have no difficulty understanding Python 2 code. To download the Python 3 interpreter, navigate to https://www.python.org/downloads/. At the top of the webpage, the correct version should be indicated. See the figure below:

Figure 1:

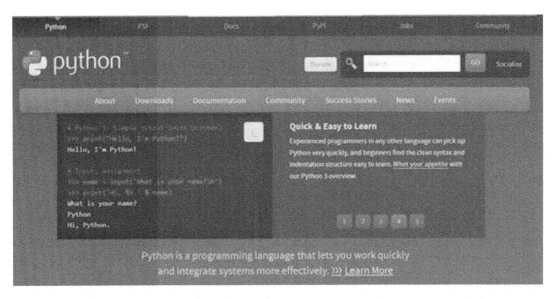

Before any programmer can proceed through the remainder of this book and begin writing their Python code, it is necessary to go through various steps for running Python, which completes the installation. Python installation will vary according to the operating system installed on your computer and the installation source you choose.

There are limited places where you can obtain information about this programming language, but we're going to focus on www.python.org to make things easier. In this chapter, we'll spend some time going over the various steps required to install the Python interpreter and more on all the major operating systems.

First, locate the one compatible with your computer's operating system. Then, follow these steps to obtain the desired results and install the Python programming language and all its associated software on your computer.

Python Installation for MacOS

MacOS is a working framework created by Apple Inc. It is the same as the Windows Operating System and another operational framework. The more significant part of the more current adaptations of MacOS has pre-installed Python. You can check whether the Python is installed or not by the accompanying directions.

Download Python 3 or 2 new types. Python 3.6 or Python 2.7 was the fresher form at the hour of writing this. Download the Mac OS X 64-piece/32-piece installer. Run the bundle and follow the installation steps to install the Python bundles.

·   Click on the "Downloads" icon from the official Python website and select Mac.

·   Click on the "Download Python 3.8.0" button to view all the downloadable files.

·   Different screen will come up, select the Python version you would like to download.

We will be using the Python 3 version under "Stable Releases." So scroll down the page and click on the "Download macOS 64-bit installer" link under Python 3.8.0, as shown in the picture below.

·   A pop-up window titled "Python3.8.0-macosx10.9.pkg" will be displayed.

·   Click the "Save File" button to download the file.

·   Once the download has completed, double-click the saved file icon, and an "Install Python" pop window will be displayed.

- Click on the "Continue" button to continue, and a terms and conditions pop-up window will be displayed.

- Click "Agree" and then click on the "Install" button.

- A notification requesting administrator permission and password will be displayed. Simply enter your system password to begin the installation.

- An "Installation was successful" message will be displayed once the installation has been completed. Click on the "Close" button, and you are all set.

- Navigate to the directory where you installed Python to verify the installation and double-click on the Python launcher icon to take you to the Python Terminal.

Python Installation for Windows

- Click on the "Downloads" icon from the official Python website and select Windows.

- Click on the "Download Python 3.8.0" button to view all the downloadable files.

- It will bring different screens to select the Python version you want to download. We will be using the Python 3 version under "Stable Releases." So scroll down the page and click on the "Download Windows x86-64 executable installer".

- A pop-up window titled "Python3.8.0-amd64.exe" will be displayed.

- Click the "Save File" button to download the file.

- Once the download has completed, double-click the saved file icon, and a "Python 3.8.0 (64-bit) Setup" pop window will be displayed.

- Make sure that you select the "Install Launcher for all users (recommended)" and the "Add Python 3.8 to PATH" checkboxes. Note—If you already have an older version of Python installed on your system, the "Upgrade Now" button will appear instead of the "Install Now" button, and neither checkboxes will be displayed.

- Click the "Install Now" button, and a "User Account Control" pop-up window will be displayed.

- A notification stating, "Do you want to allow this app to make changed to your device" will be displayed. Click on Yes.

· A new pop-up window titled "Python 3.8.0 (64-bit) Setup" will be displayed, containing a setup progress bar.

· Once the installation has been completed, a "Set was successful" message will be displayed. Click on the "Close" button, and you are all set.

· *Navigate to the directory where you installed Python to verify the installation and double-click on the Python.exe file.*

Chapter 3: How to work with Pycharm and IDLE

Once Python software is installed, you need a dedicated development environment on your system to create programs. While it is probable to work with the help of the basic IDLE that basic python installation comes with, IDEs such as Pycharm are encouraged to be used by developers for better software development workflow. IDEs provide productivity and make it easy for developers to debug their preexisting code deployed as software.

How Python IDLE Shell Works

Want to know how Python IDLE Shell works? The IDLE shell can be used for interactive Python programming. See how the IDLE Shell works in this blog post.

The IDLE Shell is a shell that operates within the main window of the IDE and has access to all of its features, including debugging and autocomplete. The program is usually opened when you load or create a Python file using the File -> New Window menu option, which will automatically launch an editor window and an idle shell window. The IDLE shell can also be used as a standalone program.

For the example, we will use IDLE version 3.6 running on Python 3.4. Type in the following code into a new file named idletest1.py:

Print ('Welcome to Python Tutorials!' +.'
' + 'Press ENTER to exit...') print('End of file.') 1 2 3 4 print ('Welcome to Python Tutorials!' + '
' + 'Press ENTER to exit...') print ('End of file.')

Save the file by selecting File -> Save and then File -> Quit, and then start the IDLE 3.6 shell by clicking on the icon at the top of the screen, showing the IDLE icon.

The Python Shell 1 window opens with a blank editor pane. This is where our Python code will be written, so no other windows are open.

Note: It is important to recall that all your code will be destroyed as soon as you exit the terminal window. Hence, we need to ensure that all our code is entered into a Python file even if we work using an IDLE.

How to Open Python Files in IDLE?

IDLE makes it easy to open and read already written Python files with a .py extension on the terminal. Remember that this command will work only when you are in the same directory of the Python file.

Program Code:

$ python sample.py

The above command will open the preexisting code for the programmers to read.

IDLE can automatically highlight unique components of your syntax

IDLE helps developers to complete code by providing hints

IDLE can easily indent code

You can also use the GUI file option to click on the 'Open' button to use any Python files on your IDLE shell. Advanced programmers, however, recommend using the path to open Python files if you are not in the same directory.

How to Edit These Files?

Once the files are opened in your IDLE, you can use your keyboard to start editing the code present in the file. As IDLE provides line numbers, it becomes easy for developers to manipulate any non-indented code. Once the file is edited, use the F5 key to execute it on your terminal code.

If there are no faults, then the output will be displayed, or else if there are errors, the traceback errors will be displayed.

While not as efficient as other advanced IDEs present in the market, Python IDLE still acts as a great debugging tool. It provides several debugging features, such as placing endpoints, catching exceptions, and parsing the code to debug the code quickly. However, it is not ideal and can cause problems if your Project library starts to grow.

Irrespective of how much less it offers, IDLE is still possibly the best developer tool for complete beginners.

Exercise:

Create a new program using the Python IDLE to add two numbers and debug the code using breakpoints. You are free to use any resources on the Internet to solve this simple problem if you are unaware of any programming components.

Integrated Development Environment(IDE)

Due to their inability to handle highly demanding projects, Python IDLE is often not recommended for real-world application development. Instead, developers are asked to manage and develop their code in unique development environments known as IDEs. IDEs provide tight integration capabilities for programmers with different libraries.

Features of IDEs

1. Easy Integration With Libraries & Frameworks

One of the many essential features of IDEs is that they can make it easy for libraries and frameworks to be easily integrated into software applications. With IDLE, you have to assign them individually every time you use them, and IDEs, however, do the hard work for you by autocompleting various import statements. Many IDEs also provide direct integration with git repositories.

2. Object Orientation Design Integration

A lot of Python programmers who develop applications use an object-oriented paradigm. Python IDLE doesn't provide any tools to make it easy for developers to create applications while following object-oriented principles. All modern IDEs offer components such as class hierarchy diagrams for developers to kickstart their projects with better programming logic.

3. Syntax Highlighting

Syntax highlighting helps programmers increase productivity and lets them not make simple, obvious mistakes. For example, you cannot use reserved keywords such as 'if' for variable names. IDE automatically recognizes this mistake and helps developers understand with the help of Syntax highlighting.

4. Code Completion

All modern IDEs use advanced artificial intelligence and machine learning techniques to automatically complete the code for developers. The IDEs collect a lot of information from your packages, suggesting different variables or methods based on your input and the logic you are writing. Even though auto-completion is a great feature, never rely entirely on it as it can sometimes mess up your program execution and give errors.

5. Version Control

Version control is one of the major headaches for developers. For example, if you use private libraries and frameworks for your application, they may sometimes get updated and make your application broken. As a developer, you should be mindful of these changes and implement new code execution for all the applications to work as it is. The version control mechanism allows developers to easily update their core application without messing up already-written code. IDEs provide direct version control with websites such as Github.

Apart from these features, IDEs can also provide advanced debugging features for developers. Pycharm and eclipse are the most popular Python IDEs for independent developers and organizations.

Pycharm

Pycharm is a Python-exclusive IDE developed by JetBrains, one of the pioneers in software tool development. Initially, Pycharm was developed by the JetBrains team to handle their IDEs for other programming languages. Due to its portable nature, later Jetbrains team released it as a separate product for users worldwide. Pycharm is available for all popular operating systems and has two variants - community and professional.

1. The community version is free and open-source software anyone can use to write Python code. However, it has limited features, especially regarding version control and third-party library Integration.

2. A professional version is a paid IDE that provides developers with advanced functionalities and many integration options. Developers can easily create web or data science applications from Pycharm IDE using the professional version.

What Are the Features Available in Pycharm?

Pycharm is popular due to its exclusive features for enthusiastic Python developers with high-quality integration capabilities.

1. Code Editor

The code editor with Pycharm is one of the finest in the industry. You will be amazed by the code completion skills whenever you work with new projects using this editor. JetBrains has used several advanced machine learning models to make the IDE intelligent enough to understand even the complex programming blocks and provide suggestions to the user.

Pycharm editor can also be customized for a better viewing experience while working a lot as a developer. Light and dark themes available for the users can help you change the composition according to your mood.

2. Code Navigation

Pycharm makes it easy for programmers to manage files with a complex and complete organization system. Special features such as bookmarks and lens mode can help Python programmers to manage their essential programming blocks and code logic effectively.

3. Advanced Refactoring

Pycharm provides advanced refactoring features for the developers to easily change file, class, or method names without breaking the program. When you refactor your code using

IDLE, it immediately breaks the code because the default Python IDLE is not intelligent enough to understand the difference between new and old names.

Most Python developers use Advanced refactoring capabilities whenever they want to update their code or migrate to a much better third-party library for one of their software components.

4. Integration With Web Technologies

Most Python developers belong to the web domain, which occupies a large portion of the software industry. Pycharm makes it easy for developers to easily integrate their software with Python web frameworks such as Django. Pycharm is also intelligent enough to understand HTML, CSS, and Javascript code web developers usually use to create web services.

All these features make it easy for Python web developers to easily integrate their existing web code into one of the Python frameworks.

5. Integration With Scientific Libraries

Pycharm is also known for its high support of scientific and advanced mathematical libraries such as Scipy and Numpy. While it can never wholly replace your data integration and cleaning setup, it can help you create a basic pseudo logic for all your data science projects.

6. Software Testing

Pycharm can perform high-level unit testing strategies for even complicated and large projects with many members. It provides advanced debugging tools and remote configuration facilities to take advantage of the Alpha and beta testing workflow.

How to Work With Pycharm?

With enough information about Pycharm, you must have already been convinced that Pycharm is an essential development tool for your local system. This section provides the information necessary for you to install Pycharm and understand how to use it to handle your Python projects better.

Step—1: Installing Pycharm

Installing Pycharm on any operating system is pretty straightforward. You must download the installation package from the official website or one of the many package managers.

Head to Jetbrains' official website and visit the downloads tab in the top right corner. Now download the executable or dmg file depending on your operating system and click on it once downloaded to follow the instructions provided on the screen.

To download a professional version of the software, you need to provide payment details first to download a trial software. Once the trial period is completed, you will be charged and can use the professional version without any problem.

Note:

For the Pycharm IDE to install successfully on your system, you must ensure that Python is installed. It automatically detects the Python path to install the software's core libraries.

Step—2: Creating New Projects

Once the software is installed, open the Pycharm IDE from your applications or use the icon on your Desktop. Once the Pycharm is opened, a new popup will open for you to start a new project from scratch. In the top left of the software interface, you will find an option to open a new project using the "File" option. Other options include importing and exporting to use existing projects or saving current working projects quickly.

Whenever you first open a project on Python, you will be asked to select the Python interpreter you want to use for all programming procedures. Select the 'virtualenv' option if you are unaware of where to find the Python interpreter, as this option will automatically search the system and find a Python interpreter for you.

Step—3: Organizing Using Pycharm

Once you start creating projects using Pycharm, creating new folders and resources for your Program files is essential to access them better.

Just click on the new --> folder option to create a new folder on your project interface. In this section, you can add any Python scripts or assets used in your software.

Whenever you create a new file in a separate folder, a file will be made with the .py extension. If you want to create different class files or templates, you must select them while explicitly creating a file in your folder.

Step—4: Advanced Features in Pycharm

Once the code is written and integrated, you can quickly run the built-in IDLE interface or the Pycharm particular output interface.

All the code you write will automatically be saved in real-time; hence, you need not worry about losing any critical project data because of a bad network connection or power loss. All you have to do is use Ctrl S or Cmd S to save a copy of a project on your local system.

Once the program is completed, you can use the Shift + F10 button to run and compile the code with the help of an interpreter.

You can search any method, variable, or snippets used in your project using Ctrl F or Cmd F commands. Just use this shortcut and enter the details that you are searching for.

Once the Python code is imported and deployed to your required operating systems, you need to start arranging a debugging project environment for constantly clearing bugs on your system. Use the Shift + F9 button to place breakpoints and solve logical problems without messing up the whole code logic or breaking the core program.

Chapter 4: What are Python Variables?

Python programs need basic building blocks such as variables and operators to make them function as they are intended to. Both variables and operators are easy for beginners to understand the programming logic that can help them create algorithms essential for the functioning of complex software.

Python Variables

For creating any program, data needs to be handled effectively. Both users and the software interact with the help of data. Without data, Software applications will not make sense and will not provide any purpose for the end-user. For the software applications to upload or download data, variables are used.

The concept of variables was first used in a mathematical field called algebra to define values. Variables are not a new addition to the Python programming language. From the inception of high-level programming languages, variables are used to store data in a specific computer memory location. Initial adopters of computer programming faced difficulties extracting data based on computer memory information. Hence, they used the concept of variables from Algebra to place values in computer memory and use them whenever they wanted.

For Example:
$2x + 3y$ is a mathematical equation.

1. If $x = 3$ and $y = 4$, then the result of the above statement will be 18.
2. If $x = 2$ and $y = 6$, then the result of the above statement will be 22.

In the same way, by using variables, you can change the program output by the literal values you give to them. All the variable values can be easily replaced. According to programming terminology, if you don't want to replace the value of a variable value, it should usually be called a constant.

To understand how variables work, you first need to know how Python program execution works. We will make it straightforward for you with the help of using a print statement.

Program Code:

Print ("This is a sample analysis.")

Output:

This is a sample analysis.

In the above example, the output will be immediately displayed when the print statement is entered on the computer screen and executed. But a lot happens backwards to reflect this output.

What Happens?

When the program is executed, it will read each line and match according to the libraries it was given access.

An interpreter often does this matching process with high parsing skills. It can not only determine what each character in the program represents but will also be able to match the variable details and pull the information that is present in this memory location to verify the program logic.

Even after complex parsing, the program will throw errors or exceptions if the interpreter cannot find the methods or variables defined.

In the above example, when the interpreter parses the print statement, it immediately recognizes that it is a core library method defined in the Python library and will output any string literals between parenthesis.

If you are entirely aware of the above explanation, it is now time to learn how variables work in Python.

Program Code:

Program = "This is a simple analysis."

print (program)

Output:

This is a simple analysis.

What Happened?

Once the program execution starts, the interpreter will usually parse all the lines of code that the programmer gives.

Instead of just seeing a print statement followed by a text block, the interpreter now observes a particular identifier known as a variable with the name 'program.' It searches the code before and finds that the variable is already defined with a text and stored at a particular memory location.

Now the interpreter will print the variable on the screen as provided by the programmer by pulling the data defined in the variable.

This is the primary mechanism with which variables work, even if they are used in complex code logic.

The variable value will be changed instantly when they are replaced. This is important for a Python programmer because all dynamic programs change variables according to the user inputs and return them even when the program runs in real time.

Program Code:

sample = "This is an example"

print(sample)

sample = "This is a second example"

print(sample)

Output:

This is an example

This is a second example

In the above example, as we know that the Python interpreter parses the code line by line sequentially, the first statement is printed with the first variable value provided, and the second print statement is published with the second variable value provided.

Naming Variables

All python programmers must follow the default guidelines provided by the Python community while creating variables. Not following these conditions will throw your programs into errors that are hard to ignore or can sometimes make your application crash. Using a specific guideline while creating programs can also improve readability.

Rules for Writing Variables:

According to Python guidelines, you can only use numbers, alphabetical characters, and an underscore to create variable names. For example, 'sample1' can be used as a variable name, whereas '$sample1' cannot be used as a variable name because it is started with an unsupported symbol $.

Python programmers cannot start a variable name with a number. For example, 'sample1' is a supported variable naming format, whereas '1sample' is not supported.

Python programmers cannot use reserved words allotted for various programming routines used for Python development. Currently, 33 reserved keywords are inaccessible for developers to use as identifiers while creating real-world applications with Python. For example, 'for' is a reserved keyword.

While this is not a rigid rule, it is always good to follow a simple variable naming method for better readability. Creating complex or confusing variable names can make your code look unpolished. While this practice suits high-level languages such as C, C++ and Pearl, Python doesn't endorse this philosophy.

How to Define Variables?

All the variables defined in Python programming language use the assignment operator (=) to initiate a value to the variable first.

Syntax Format:
Nameofthevariable = valueofthevariable

For Example:

example = 343

This is a variable with an integer data type

example1 = " Russia"

This is a variable with a string data type

An example is the name of the variable we have created, and 343 is the variable value we have given during its initiation.

Look at the variable-defining method above, where we did not explicitly mention any variable data type because Python is intelligent enough to understand the varying data types automatically.

How to Find the Memory Address of Variables?

All variables are stored in a specific memory location. Whenever you call the variable name, the Python interpreter will pull the information present in this memory location. If you ask the Python interpreter to replace the variable, it will just remove the already placed variable value and replace it with the new variable value. The old variable value will be deleted or stored using a garbage mechanism for future use cases.

Usually, programming languages such as C use pointers to quickly determine and pull the information about the variable's memory location. However, Python doesn't support pointers as it is often challenging to implement and needs a lot of compilation skills that the interpreter is usually unaware of.

Instead, Python developers can use the built-in id() function to get the memory address of the variable easily.

Program Code:

sample = 64

First, create a variable of your favorable data type

id(first)

Now call using this built-in function called id()

Output:

1x37372829x

Here, 1x37372829x is the memory location of the variable in hexadecimal format.

Using the method below, you can now replace the variable and check whether the id() has been changed or not.

Program Code:

sample = 64

id(sample)

sample = 78

Now, we have replaced the variable value with a new one

id(sample)

This will again print the output of the memory location address

Output:

1x37372829x

If you have observed, the memory location did not change, but with a small print verification, you can see that the variable value is changed.

Program Code:

```python
sample = 64

id (sample)

sample = 78

print(sample)
```

Output:

78

Local and Global Variables in Python

According to your writing programming logic, variables can be local and global. In theory, local variables can be used in only particular methods or classes that you want them to be used. In contrast, global variables can be used in any part of the program without any problems. When you call a local variable outside a specific function, you will usually be thrown an error by the Python interpreter.

Program Code:

```python
# This is a function example with a local variable

def sample():

example = " This is a trail"

print(example)
```

Output:

This is a trail

This example defines the variable as a local variable inside a function. Hence, it will throw a traceback error whenever you call it inside any function, as shown below.

Program Code:

This is a function example with a local variable

def sample():

      example = " This is a trail"
      print(example)

def secondsample():

      print(example)

This is a second method we have initiated

  Output:

This is a trail

Traceback error: variable not defined

On the other hand, global variables can be used to initiate variables for the whole program.

Program Code:

example = "This is a trail"

A global variable has been created

def sample():

      print(example)

def secondsample():

      print(example)

This is a second method we have initiated

Output:

This is a trail

This is a trail

As both functions can access global variables, two print statements are provided as an output on the computer screen.

Note:
Deciding which type of variables to use is entirely your choice. Many programmers heavily depend on local variables to run their applications faster. On the other hand, global variables can be used if you don't want to be overwhelmed with a lot of memory management.

Chapter 5: **Python Basics**

Python programmers must ensure that to make applications dynamic. All their applications need to take input directly from the user and provide output according to their inputs. Python interpreter and all the functions in your program can access these input values provided by the user.

In this chapter, we will deliver a few example programs to help you understand how to improve the user experience for the software you have created based on the input and output operations.

Why Are Input Values Necessary?

Input values are what make applications survive. Everything runs from web applications to the latest metaverse applications with the help of input values provided by the user. For example, when you log in to Facebook, you must enter your email address and password. These are inputs, and your account will be authenticated only if the provided information is correct.

Even advanced applications such as facial recognition technology use face data points as input. Every real-world application these days asks for and collects user input data to provide a better user experience.

Use Cases:
Let us suppose there is a Python application you have developed for a mature audience; hence, it cannot be used by people below 18 years old.

We can use conditional input verification for the above scenario by asking the user to enter their age. If the age is above 18, the application will become accessible to the user. On the other hand, If the age is below 18, the application will not be accessible to the user. Python takes inputs from all the supported data types to determine whether or not someone can access your software. This is just one real-world example. There are countless applications you can perform by accessing input from your end users.

Python Comments

When programming teams work on complex and highly demanding projects, a lot must be exchanged between different team programmers to understand the project's essence. Comments help programmers to pass information without messing with the program quickly.

When a programmer uses comments, the Python interpreter will ignore the comments provided and will go over to the following line. As Python has a lot of open source projects, comments help developers easily understand how to integrate third-party libraries and frameworks into their code.

Comments can also help your code readable and hence better understandable. While it may seem unnecessary for certain programmers to remember the code logic they have written, you will be surprised by how much programmers forget the code logic they have written. Having specific insights about how you have written the code logic will be great for future reference.

Python supports two types of comments for programmers to write between their code.

1. Single Line Comments

Single-line comments are the most popular type of comments used by Python programmers as they can be easily written between code.

You need to use the '#' symbol to use single-line comments. The interpreter will ignore anything that is followed by this symbol.

Program Code:

#This is an example of a single-line comment that is followed by a hash symbol

print ("This is just an example ")

Output:

This is just an example.

Because of using a single-line comment, the interpreter ignored it and executed just the print statement.

Why Are Single—Line Comments Used?

Single-line comments are primarily used in the middle of the code to help other programmers understand how the program logic works and details the functions of the implemented variables.

2. Multiline Comments

While it is entirely possible to use single-line comments to write three or four lines of continuous comments, it is not recommended because Python provides a better way to annotate multi-line comments.

As shown below, python programmers can use string literals to create multi-line comments.

Program Code:

```
"""
This is a comment
In Python
with multiple lines
Author: Python Rookie """
print ("This is just an example ")
```

Output:

This is just an example.

Like single-line comments, only the print statement is executed when you execute the above program.

Why Are Multiline Comments Used?

Programmers often use multiline comments to define license details or explain comprehensive information about different packages and methods with various implementation examples. The programmers who are reading the code can understand it effectively.

Reserved Keywords

Reserved keywords are the default keywords for a programming language that programmers cannot use as identifiers while writing their code. Identifiers are usually used for variables, class and function names.

When you use a reserved keyword in your program, the interpreter will not allow it and throw an error. For example, if you use 'for' for one of your variables will not work because 'for' is usually used to define a specific type of loop structure in Python programming.

There are 33 reserved keywords that you cannot use in your programs. As a python programmer, it is highly suggested to know not to make unnecessary errors while creating complex projects.

Exercise:
To get familiar with the Python commands we have explained before, try to find the reserved keywords in Python by yourself using the Python terminal.

Computer programmers usually use operators to combine literal and form statements or expressions.

Example:
$$2x + 3z = 34$$
Here 2x, 3z and 34 are literals, whereas + and = are operators used on these literals to form an expression.

Exercises

Write a Python program to get input from the user. Using this input, use different arithmetic operators such as multiplication and division. You can also try to find the remainder.

Create a Python print() statement with a poem of your choice.

Create a Python program that encourages Unicode developers to write code with good functionality.

Write a Python program to convert a decimal number to a hexadecimal number.

Write a Python program that takes in inputs three numbers, x, y and z and computes the value of x^2 (2y + 5z).

Chapter 6: What are Python Data Types?

Python programmers use many data types to create universal applications on different platforms. A python programmer needs to understand the importance of data types in software development.

What Are Data Types?

To be precise, data types are a set of an already predefined range of values that programmers use while creating variables. It is also vital to recollect that as Python is not a statically typed language, it is not required to define data types of variables explicitly. All statically typed languages such as C and C++ will usually ask programmers to define the data types of variables.

While Python programmers are not forced to define them to create programs, it is still an essential prerequisite for programmers to learn about different available data types to develop complex programs that can interact with users efficiently.

Here is an example of a statically typed language and how they define variables.

Program Code:

int age = 12:

Here, int is the data type that is defined. Age is the name of the variable created, and 12 is the value provided to be stored in the age variable.

On the other hand, Python defines a variable without explicitly defining the variable type, as shown below.

Program Code:

age = 12

Here, age and the value are provided. Still, the data type is not defined because the Python interpreter is already capable enough to understand that the value provided is an integer.

Understanding Data Types

Popular data types that Python programmers use in their applications.

Python Strings

Strings are data types usually used to represent a bunch of text. Programmers can use String data types to represent text in a program by linking them with single quotes. Whenever a string data type is created, an 'str' object is designed with a sequence of characters.

Humans usually communicate with each other in the text; hence, strings are the most critical data types developers need to be aware of to create meaningful software. It is also essential to represent data in strings because computers always understand data in binary; hence, using ASCII and Unicode encoding mechanisms is vital.

Python 3 has introduced an advanced encoding mechanism to understand foreign languages such as Chinese, Japanese and Korean, making the usage of Strings essential for software development.

How are strings represented?

x = 'This is an example'

print (x)

Output:

This is an example

Everything in between the single quotes belongs to a string data type. This string data is defined using a variable 'x.' The memory location and size of the variable with a string data type are usually determined by the number of bits a variable occupies. The number of characters in a string data type is directly proportional to the number of bits.

For example, in the above example, 'This is an example' has 18 characters, along with the whitespaces.

There are several other ways to define strings for you as a Python programmer. For consistency, always use a single type according to your convenience while working on real-world projects.

Program Code:

a = " This is an example"

#Using double quotes to define strings

print(a)

b = "' This is an example '"

Using three single quotes to define strings

print(b)

c = """ This is an example

 but with more than one line """

print(c)

Output:

This is an example

This is an example

This is an example but with more than one line

In the above example program, we have defined three ways to define strings. You can also use special characters, symbols, and new tab lines between quotes. Python supports escape sequences that are used by all other programming languages. For example, \n is an escape sequence popular with programmers to create new lines.

How to Access Characters in Strings?

As strings are the most used data types in Python, the core library provides several inbuilt functions that can be used to relate with the string data effectively.

You need to know the index numbers to access characters in a string. Index numbers usually start with 0 instead of 1. You can also use negative indexing and slicing operations to access a part of a string.

Example:

first = 'Programming'

We can now access characters from the string

print (' Example used =', first)

Will print the whole string

print ('first character =' , first[0])

Will print the first character

print ('last character =' , first[-1])

#Will print the last character using negative indexing

print ('last character =' , first[10])

#Will print the last character using positive indexing

print ('Sliced character =' , first[0:2])

Will print the sliced character from zero to the third index.

Output:

Example used = Programming

first character = P

last character = g

Last character = g

Sliced character = Pro

As all the string data types are immutable, replacing characters in a literal string is impossible. If you try to replace string characters, it will give a Type error as an output.

Program Code:

first = 'programming'

first[1] = 'c'

print(first)

Output:

TypeError – You can't replace string characters

Python String Formatters

You might want to print variables alongside a string at times. You can use commas or string formatters to achieve the same result.

>>> city='Ahmedabad'

>>> print("Age",21,"City",city)

Output

Age 21 City Ahmedabad

1. f-strings

The letter ' f precedes the string,' and the variables are mentioned in curly braces in their respective positions.

>>> name='Ayushi'

>>> print(f"It isn't {name}'s birthday")

Output

It is not Ayushi's birthday

Because we wanted two single marks in the string, we used double quotes to delimit the entire series.

2. format() technique

You may perform the same thing with the format() technique. It comes after the string and has the variables separated by commas as arguments.

To position, the variables in the string, use curly brackets. You can put 0,1,... or the variables inside the curly brackets.

When implementing the latter, you must use the formatting technique to assign values to them.

```
1.    >>> print("I love {0}".format(a))
```

Output

```
I love dogs
```

```
1.    >>> print("I love {a}".format(a='cats'))
```

Output

```
I love cats
```

The variables do not have to be defined before the print statement.

>>> print("I love {b}".format(b='ferrets'))

Output
I love ferrets

3. % operator

In a string, the percent operator goes where the variables go. The letter s stands for a string in percents.

The variables and operator follow the string in parentheses/in a tuple.

```
1.  >>> b='ferrets'
2.  >>> print("I love %s and %s" %(a,b))
```

Output

```
I love dogs and cats
```

Other options include:

%f – for floating-point numbers

%d – for integers

String Manipulation Techniques

Strings are the most used data types, and hence Python core library offers several manipulation techniques that programmers can take advantage of. Understanding string manipulation techniques can help you quickly extract data from a large pool of information. Data scientists should be more aware of these techniques.

1. Concatenate

Concatenate refers to joining two separate entities. With this procedure, two strings can be joined together using the arithmetic operator '+.' If you want better readability with strings, you can just use whitespaces in between the two strings.

Program Code:

example = 'This is' + 'a great example'

print (example)

Output:

This is a great example

Remember that when you concatenate, whitespaces are not given. You need to add whitespaces on your own while connecting, as shown below.

Program Code:

Example = 'This is' + ' ' + ' a great example'

Output:

This is a great example

2. Multiply

When you use the String multiply technique, your string value will be repeated continuously. To multiply string content, we can use the * operator. *

Program Code:

example = ' Great' * 4 *

print(example)

Output:

Great Great Great Great

3. Appending

With the help of this operation, you can add any string to the end of one string by using the arithmetic operator +=. Remember that the appended string will only be added to the end of the string but not in the middle.

Program Code:

example = " France is a beautiful country "

example + = " You need to visit at least once"

print (example)

Output:

France is a beautiful country you need to visit at least once

4. Length

Apart from using string operations, you can also use prebuilt functions in the core library to do additional tasks to your code. For example, a string's length() function will help you find the number of characters in a string.

Note: Blank Space will also be added as a character in the string.

Program Code:

Example = ' Today it will rain "

ptint(len(example))

Output:

18

5. Find

When you use strings as your primary data type, there will be several instances where you need to find a part of the string. You can use the inbuilt find() function to solve this problem. The output will provide the first time the output is found with an index for the position so you can verify.

Note: Python interpreter will provide only positive indexes when you use the find() function

Program Code:

Example = " This is great"

Sample = example.find('gr')

print(sample)

Output:

9

If the substring is not found, the interpreter will provide an output of value -1.

Program Code:

example = " This is great"

sample = example.find('f')

print(sample)

Output:

-1

6. Lower and higher case

You can use lower() and higher() functions to convert characters in a string to the lower or higher case completely.

Program Code:

example = " China is the most populous country"

sample = lower.example()

print(sample)

Output:

China is the most populous country.

Program Code:

example = " China is the most populous country"

sample = higher.example()

print(sample)

Output:

CHINA IS THE MOST POPULOUS COUNTRY

7. title

You can use the title() function to change string format to camel case format.

Program Code:

example = " China is the most populous country"

sample = title.example()

print(sample)

Output:

China Is The Most Populous Country

Integers

Integers are particular data types that Python supports to include integer numbers in Python code. Numerical values are needed for performing arithmetic operations or to provide details about a statistical value.

When a Python interpreter sees a data value with an integer type, it will immediately create an int object with the value provided. All int object values can be replaced whenever the developer wants to, as these values are not immutable.

Developers use 'int' data types for creating several complex features in their software. For example, the pixel density value for an image or video file is usually represented using integers.

Note:

A developer needs to be aware of unary operators (+,-) that can be used to represent positive and negative integers, respectively. For positive integers, you need not specify the unary operator, but for negative integers, the inclusion of an operator is a must.

Program Code:

x = 25

y = -45

```
print(x)
```

print(y)

Output:

25

-45

Python supports large numerical values up to ten digits. While most real-world applications do not create bottleneck situations because of higher numerical values, you still need to ensure that no huge integers are involved.

Floating—Point numbers

Not all numerical values are integers. You may occasionally need to deal with data that have a decimal value. Python makes sure developers deal with this data with the help of floating-point numbers. You can deal with decimal values with as long as ten decimal points with floating-point numbers.

Program Code:

```
x = 4.2324324
```

```
y = 67.32323
```

```
print(x)
```

print(y)

Output:

4.2324324

67.32323

You can also use floating-point numbers to represent data using hexadecimal notation.

Program Code:

```
A = float.hex(23.232)
```

print(A)

Output:

0x367274872489

A lot of python programmers also use floating-point data types to represent complex and exponential numbers.

Booleans

Finally, let's talk about Booleans. A Boolean data type is another Python data type.

1. The value of a Boolean expression

What are Boolean values?

A Boolean value can be either True or False, as we saw earlier. Isalpha() and issubset(), for example, yield a Bo, 2}): 3}

2. Declaring a Boolean expression

You can declare a Boolean the same way as you would an integer.

d>>> days=True

We didn't need to use quotations to delimit the True value, as you can see. If you do that, you'll get a string instead of a Boolean.

Also, we have reallocated a Boolean to what was previously a set.

```
>>> type('True')
```

Output
<class 'str'>

3. The bool() function

The bool() function, as we've seen before, turns another value into a Boolean type.

```
>>> bool('Wisdom')
```

Output
True

```
>>> bool([])
```

Output

False

4. Different Constructs' Boolean Values

Distinct values have different Boolean equivalents. We use the bool() Python set technique to find the values in this example.

```
1.   >>> bool(0)
```

Output

```
False
```

1 has a Boolean value of True, and so does 0.00000000001.

```
1.   >>> bool(0.000000000001)
```

Output

```
True
```

The Boolean value of 0 is False, for example.

A string has a Boolean value of True, but an empty string has False.

```
>>> bool(' ')
```

Output

True

```
>>> bool('')
```

Output

False

Any empty construct has a Boolean value of False, and a non-empty one has

Output

True.

```
>>> bool(())
Output
False
>>> bool((1,3,2))
Output
True
```

5. Boolean operations

a. Arithmetic algorithm

A set can be subjected to some mathematical operations. It takes a value of 0 for False and 1 for True and then applies the operator to both.

- Addition

Two or more Booleans can be added. Let's have a look at how that goes.

```
>>> True+False #1+0

Output
1

>>> True+True #1+1

Output
2

>>> False+True #0+1

Output
1

>>> False+False #0+0
```

- **Multiplication and Subtraction**

The same method is adopted for multiplication and subtraction.

```
>>> False-True
```

53

Output

-1

- Division

Let's try dividing Booleans.

>>> False/True

Output

0.0

Remember that division results in afloat.

>>> True/False

```
Traceback (most recent call last):File "<pyshell#148>", line 1, in <module>
True/False
ZeroDivisionError: division by zero
```

This was a one-time occurrence. In a subsequent session, we'll learn more about exceptions.

- Exponentiation, Modulus, and Floor Division

Modulus, exponentiation, and floor division all follow the same laws.

>>> False%True

>>> True**False

Output

1

>>> False**False

Output

1

>>> 0//1

Try your combinations like the one below.

>>> (True+True)*False+True

Output

1

b. Relational

So far, we've learned the relational operators >, <, >=, <=, !=, and ==. All of these things are true for Boolean values.

Output

```
False
```

```
1    >>> False<=True
```

Output

```
True
```

We will give you a few instances, but you should try them all.

This assumes False has a value of 0 and True has a value of 1.

c. Bitwise

Bitwise operators typically operate bit by bit. The following code, for example, ORs the bits 2(010) and 5(101), yielding seven as a result (111).

```
>>> 2|5
```

Output

```
7
```

The bitwise operators, on the other hand, also apply to Booleans. Let's have a look at how.

It returns True only if values are True.

```
1.   >>> True&False
```

Output

```
False
```

```
1.   >>> True&True
```

Output

True

Because Booleans are single-bit, these operations are identical to applying them to 0 and/or

Bitwise |

If both variables are False, it returns False.

>>> False|True

Output

True

Bitwise XOR (^)

This will only return True if one of the values is True and the other is False.

>>> **False**^True

Output

True

>>> **False**^False

Output

```
False
```

```
1.    >>> True^True
```

Output

```
False
```

Binary 1's Complement

This calculates 1's complement for True(1) and False(0).

>>> ~True

OUTPUT

Left-shift(<<) and Right-shift(>>) Operators

As discussed earlier, these operators shift the value by specified number of bits left and right, respectively.

```
-2
```

```
1.    >>> ~False
```

Output

```
-1
```

```
1.    >>> False>>2
2.    >>> True<<2
```

Output

4

One is true. When two places to the left are shifted, the result is 100, binary for four. As a result, it yields 4.

d. Identity

For Booleans, the identity operators 'is' and 'is not applicable.

```
1.    >>> False is False
```

Output

```
True
```

```
1.    >>> False is 0
```

Output

```
False
```

e. Logical

Finally, logical operators work with Booleans.

>>> False and True

Output

False

Chapter 7: Data Structures in Python

Python programmers often need to deal with a lot of data, and hence using variables all the time is not a recommended option. Especially Data Scientists who often need to deal with a ton of data may become overwhelmed with the amount of dynamic data they are dealing with. To help programmers who work on complex and data-demanding projects, it is essential to utilize the lists option Python provides in its core library. These are similar to data structures like Arrays available in core programming languages like C and C++.

Understanding several data structures that Python provides and learning techniques to add or modify data using these data structures is an essential prerequisite for a Python programmer.

Lists

The list is a Python data type that supports adding different data types in sequential order. Lists have all the properties that variables possess. They can be easily replaced, passed, or manipulated with the Python core library's help with several methods.

Lists are usually represented in Python, as shown below:

[32, 33, 34]

Here 32, 33, and 34 are the list elements. It is also essential to understand that all the list elements are of integer data type and are not defined explicitly because the Python interpreter can detect their data types.

If you observe, lists start and end with a square bracket in the above format. All the elements in the list will also be separated using a comma. It is also important to note that if the elements in a list are of string data type, then they are usually enclosed within quotes. All the elements within a particular list can also be called items.

Example:

[Nevada, Ohio, Colorado]

Here Nevada, Ohio, and Colorado are called elements of the list.

All the lists can be assigned to a variable, as shown below, with an example.

sample = ['Nevada', 'Ohio', 'Colorado']

The list will be printed like any other data type whenever you print the variable.

Program Code:

sample

Output:

[Nevada, Ohio, Colorado]

Empty List

If no elements exist in a Python list, it can be called an empty list. An empty list is also usually called a null list.

It is usually represented as [].

Program Code:

>>> example = []

This is an empty Python list.

Index in Lists

Python provides an easy way to manipulate or replace the elements in a list, specifically with the help of the usage of indexes. Indexes usually start with 0 and provide Python programmers with many functions, such as slicing and searching, to ensure that the programs work well.

Let us suppose that there is a list that we have used before

['Ohio', 'Nevada', 'Colorado']

We will print each of the indexes on the computer screen.

Program Code:

>>> example = ['Ohio', 'Nevada', 'Colorado']

>>> example[0]

>>> example [1]

>>> example [2]

Output:

Ohio

Nevada

Colorado

When the Python interpreter detects 0 as an index in the above example, it will print the first element. As the index increases, the position on the list also increases.

We can also call the items in the list as shown below, along with a string literal.

Program Code:

example = ['Ohio', 'Nevada', 'Colorado']

print(example [2] + ' is a great city')

While calling lists, an index error will be given as output if you provide an index value higher than the list elements present.

Program Code:

example = ['Ohio', 'Nevada', 'Colorado']

print(example[3])

Output:

Index error: list index out of range

Note: It is also vital to remember that you cannot use the floating-point number as an index value

Program Code:

```
example = ['Ohio', 'Nevada', 'Colorado']
print(example[ 3.2])
```

Output:

TypeError: You cannot use a floating-point index as an index value

All lists can have other lists as their elements, as shown below. All the lists inside a list are known as child lists.

Program Code:

```
x = [1,223,2,45,63,22]
print(x)
```

Output:

[1, 223, 2, 45, 63, 22]

You can call the elements in the child list using the 'list [ ][ ]' format.

Program Code:

```
x = [1,223,2,45,63,22]
print(x[0:3][2])
```

Output:

2

As in the above example, the third element in the second list is 22, and it is shown as output.

You can call the elements in a list also using the negative index. Usually, -1 refers to the last index, whereas -2 refers to the element before the last element.

Program Code:

example = ['Ohio', 'Nevada', 'Colorado']

print(example[-1])

Output:

Colorado

Tuples

Even though lists are famous data structures that Python programmers often use in their applications, they still have several problems while implementing them. As all the lists that can be created using Python are mutual objects, it becomes easy to replace, delete or manipulate them.

As a Software developer, you may need to maintain immutable lists that cannot be manipulated in any way. This is where tuples come into the discussion. It is not possible to change initiated elements in any way within Tuples. A " Type Error" will be shown as the output whenever you try to change the content within a tuple.

Program Code:

example = ('Earth' , 'Venus' , 'Mars')

print(example)

 # Creating a tuple using Python

Output:

('Earth', 'Venus', 'Mars')

In the above example, we just initiated a tuple and used a print function to output it onto the screen.

Note:

Remember that, unlike lists, tuples are not represented using square brackets but instead using parenthesis to differentiate them from lists easily.

To understand how tuples work, try to change an element from the above example and print the tuple to observe what happens.

Program Code:

example = ('Earth' , 'Venus' , 'Mars')

print(example)

Creating a tuple using Python

example[2] = 'Jupiter'

print(example)

 # Printing tuple details after an element is replaced

Output:

('Earth', 'Venus', 'Mars')

TypeError: 'tuple' object does not support item assignment

In the above example, the interpreter will throw an error to the developer as soon as an element of a tuple is changed. This proves that all the elements in a tuple are immutable and cannot be replaced, deleted, or added.

Concatenating Tuples

Like the many list operations we have performed, we can use Tuples to work on specific operations.

For example, just like lists, you can add or multiply the elements in a tuple using Python.

Program Code:

sample1 = (45,34,23)

sample2 = (32,12,11)

print(sample1 + sample2)

We are now adding two tuples

Output:

(45,34,23,32,12,11)

In the above example, two tuples are concatenated using the Addition operator. In the same way, you can use the multiplication operator to increase the elements in your tuple quickly.

We can also place other tuples inside a tuple. This process is usually known as nesting tuples.

Program Code:

A = (23, 32,12)

B = ('Tokyo', 'Paris', 'Washington')

C = (A,B)

print(C)

Output:

((23,32,12) , ('Tokyo' , ' Paris' , 'Washington'))

In the above example, two tuples are nested in another tuple.

Replication

Programmers can also repeat the values when dealing with lists using the * operator.

Program Code:

A = (2,3,4) * 3

print(A)

Output:

(2,3,4,2,3,4,2,3,4)

As said, it is impossible to change tuples' values as they are designed to be immutable. Let us check what will happen if we try to replace one value with another.

Program Code:

x = (32,64,28)

x[2] = 12

print(x)

Output:

TypeError: A tuple element cannot be replaced

Slicing With Tuples

It is possible to easily slice a part of the tuple with the help of the slicing technique that uses indexes to extract a part of the tuple.

Program Code:

x = (12,13,14,15,16)

print(x [1:3])

Output:

(13,14,15)

How to Delete a Tuple?

It is impossible to delete a specific element in a tuple, but it is possible to delete it entirely using the below command.

Program Code:

x = (12,13,14,15,16)

del x

print(x)

Output:

NameError: name 'x' is not defined

Dictionaries

In many coding languages, composite data types can be represented as dictionaries. This is true in Python as well. A dictionary can have multiple data elements of different types. You would use a dictionary to describe some real-world object. For example, you could be developing a database that represents people, with each element tracking name, age, weight, or whatever you can think of. The point is that it might have data values that are different types, and each dictionary element represents a structured data type.

Dictionaries are indicated in Python using curly braces. Elements of a dictionary are not just data points. Otherwise, we could just make up a list. Instead, they have keys and values. Dictionaries are unordered in contrast to lists and tuples.

Elements of a dictionary are specified in the form key: value. This is best illustrated using an example.

student_dict = {'Name':'Sally','ID':'A781B435','Major':'Sociology'}

You can reference the value of a given key by referencing it.

>>> print student_dict['Name']

Sally

You can reference multiple keys at once:

>>> print student_dict['Name']," is majoring in ",student_dict['Major']

Sally is majoring in Sociology

If you want to see one of your dictionaries and find out how many elements are found in that dictionary, then the best command to work with is length.

>>> len(student_dict)

3

This command can give you the number of elements in any complex data type. So you can use it with lists and tuples as well.

>>> len(readings)

7

This tells us that the reading list has seven elements.

You can create lists and tuples where the individual elements are dictionaries. This allows the creation of more complicated data types. For example, we can have a list of students.

>>> student_dict2 = {'Name':'Joe','ID':'GH7583','Major':'Business'}

>>> mystudents = [student_dict,student_dict2]

>>> mystudents[0]

{'Major': 'Sociology', 'Name': 'Sally', 'ID': 'A781B435'}

Here is how you would look up the value of an element in the list of dictionaries for a specific key:

>>> mystudents[1]['Name']

'Joe'

>>> mystudents[1]['Major']

'Business'

Exercises

Write a Python program to create a matrix using lists and provide an inverse matrix.

Write a Python program to form a few lists that interact with each other to play a word scrambling game.

Write a Python program to reverse all elements in the list and find out the character length of all the strings in the list

Write a Python program to effectively ascend or descend the values and critical pairs present in a dictionary

Write a Python program to invert a dictionary and replace its elements with the RGB values of Blue, Green, and Orange colors.

Chapter 8: Conditional Statements and Loops

Any computer program needs to make decisions for real-world usage. For example, a mobile application with advanced software will use your inputs to show whatever you want. The user makes decisions while browsing a mobile or web application.

To ensure that your programs, when written in Python, mimic these conditions, you need to be aware of conditionals and loops. These are high-level programming structures that can make your python programs more effective.

Control Flow Statements

With enough knowledge about comparison operators, you are now all set to learn about different control statements that are an essential prerequisite for enthusiastic Python developers. Programmers usually use control flow statements to write uncomplicated code for beginners.

Sequential Structure

In a sequential structure, all the steps in your program will usually be executed linearly. A lot of programs follow a sequential structure not to create complicated code. However, programmers need a lot of skill to create sequential code as it is often challenging to develop programming logic with a linear approach.

Example:

a = 34

print (a + " is my favorite number")

Output:

34 is my favorite number

In the above example, the Python interpreter parsed the code line by line linearly to give an output.

Conditional Structure

The conditional structure is a famous programming structure used to execute only a part of the program and skip the remaining logical code depending on the conditional statements.

In a conditional structure, only partial statements are executed and help Python interpreters save a lot of time by not letting it parse all the code.

If and if-else conditional structures are famous conditional branches that Python programmers use.

Looping Structure

Looping structures can be used if you want to implement the same statement or programming logic in a program again and again based on logical conclusions. Python interpreter allows you to execute a programming step repeatedly until the condition is satisfied.

Developers need to write both loop starting and termination logic to utilize the looping structure better.

While and for loop are the famous looping structures that Python programmers can experiment with within their code.

The if-Else Statement

Following the logic of the *if* statement, an *else* statement can be added to provide an alternative command, given the condition set in the first line of code is not True. This means that using the *else* statement; there's no need to specify a new condition as the statement is based on the condition set by *if*. The *else* statement will thus only run *if* the conditional statement is not True.

Note that the *else* conditional statement is optional.

If condition:
   action
Else:

   action

Example 2

```
x = 7
if x % 2 == 0:
    print("x is even")
else:
    print("x is odd")

Out: x is odd
```

In exceptional cases where both the *if* and *else* conditions hold True, the Python interpreter automatically activates the first condition and leaves the code below unread. This means the second condition set by *else* is never triggered, and there's no corresponding output.

The Elif Statement

Similar to the else condition, you can also add *elif* (which means "else if") as another optional conditional statement before adding a final *else* statement.

If condition:
   action
Elif condition:
   action
Else:

   action
Let's review a basic example.

Example 3

```
x = 10
if (x <9):
    print("small")
elif(x <12):
    print("medium")
else:
    print("large")


Out: medium
```

As the *if* conditional statement failed, the Python interpreter moves to the *elif* statement, which is True, thereby printing "*medium*".

Let's use modulo division to review another example.

Example 4

```
x = 5
if x % 2 == 0:
    print("x is divisible by 2")
elif x % 3 == 0:
    print("x is divisible by 3")
else:
    print("x is not divisible by 2 or 3")


Out: x is not divisible by 2 or 3
```

In this example, both the *if* and *elif* conditional statements are False, activating the final *else* condition.

Lastly, it's important to mention that you can write more than one *elif* statement to achieve the goals of your program.

Example 5

```
x = 5
if x % 2 == 0:
    print("x is divisible by 2")
elif x % 3 == 0:
    print("x is divisible by 3")
elif x % 5 ==0:
    print("x is divisible by 5")
else:
    print("x is not divisible by 2, 3 or 5")

Out: x is divisible by 5
```

In this example, the first *elif* condition isn't triggered, allowing a chance for the second *elif* condition to be activated successfully.

For Loops

Just like conditionals, looping structures are building blocks for Python software. Instead of checking a condition constantly, you can loop it with the help of a for or while loop.

A for loop can be applied to all data structures, such as lists, tuples, and dictionaries.

Syntax:

> For val in list:
> > { Enter the body of a loop here }
>
> The for loop can go through all the elements when a condition is given.

Example:

x = [32,12,11]

sample = 0

for val in x:

```
    sample = sample + val
```

print ("The sum of numbers is ", sample)

Output:

The sum of the numbers is 55

Instead of using arithmetical operations on every element in the list, we have just used a for loop to automate this procedure in the above example.

The While Loop

This while loop will be the type of loop we will use if we want to ensure our code will go through the cycle at least a minimum number of times. You can set how many times you would like the loop to happen when you are writing out the code to ensure that the loop will go through the process for as long as you need it.

With this kind of loop in Python, your goal will not be to have the code go through a cycle an indefinite number of times, but you do want to make sure that it can do it a specific number of times, the amount that will ensure your code works how you would like. If you want to have the program count from one to 50, you want to ensure that this program will head through the loop 50 times to finish it all off. With this option, the loop will go through the process a minimum of one time and then will check out whether the conditions of that loop have been met or not. It will put up the number one, check whether this output meets the requirements, see that it does not, put in the number 2, and continue this loop until it considers that it is at a number higher than 50.

This is a simple kind of loop that we can work with, and we will see how we can put it to practical use for some of the work we want to do. Let's look at some of the sample codes of a while loop and see what is going to happen when it gets to work:

```
counter = 1

while(counter <= 3):
```

```
principal = int(input("Enter the principal amount:"))

numberofyears = int(input("Enter the number of years:"))

rateofinterest = float(input("Enter the rate of interest:"))

simpleinterest = principal numberofyears rateofinterest/100

print("Simple interest = %.2f" %simpleinterest)

#increase the counter by 1

counter = counter + 1

print("You have calculated simple interest for three-time!")
```

Before we move on, take this code and add it to your compiler and let it execute this code. You will see that when this is done, the output will come out so that the user can place any information they want into the program. Then the program will do its computations and figure out the interest rates and the final amounts based on whatever numbers the user placed into the system. With this example, we set the loop up to go through 3 times. This allows the user to put in results three times to the system before moving on. You can always change this around and add in more of the loops if it works best for your program.

Exercises

Write a Python program to list numbers up to 2,000, divisible by 12 and multiples by 5. Use separators while listing out the elements.

Write a Python program that can convert pounds into kilograms using both for and while loop.

Using Python, create a random number generator in a number range (1,000 to 10,000).

Use loops to print at least five rangoli patterns using the alphabet

Using the continue statement, create a Python program that can complete the Fibonacci sequence

Write a Python program using loops to convert USD to EUR and GBP.

Write a Python program that can verify the password authenticity of your input. Make sure you follow password standards to verify them.

Chapter 9: How To Create Modules And Function

Python programming supports different programming paradigms. The functional programming paradigm is the most popular of the different programming paradigms available for developers to write their code. Functional programming is versatile and easy to implement for simple projects requiring fewer developers to complete the code. The functional paradigm is also considered universal due to its faster implementation of various programming components.

Creating programs with the help of functions is tricky as you always need to call the function within the program. Learning functional programming with the help of a few examples can help you create complex programs with less code.

A Real-World Example of Functions:
Functions are first used in mathematics to solve complex problems in discrete mathematics easily. Later, programmers started implementing this concept to reuse the already written code without rewriting it.

Let us use a simple mobile application to help you understand how functions work in real-world applications.

Picsart is a popular mobile photo editing application that provides several filters and tools for users to manipulate images. For example, the crop tool helps users to crop their pictures easily.

Now, when the developers of Picsart create code, they usually use different libraries, frameworks, and many functions. For example, cropping needs a separate function as it involves many complex tasks to divide pixels and provide output to the user.

Let us suppose that the developers wanted to update the application with support to crop videos. Currently, there are two options available for programmers.

1. They can create a cropping function right from scratch.
2. They can use the cropping function created for photos and add additional functionalities.

Many developers prefer the second option because it is easy and saves time. Creating functions is not as easy as we explained in the above example. It takes a lot of complex logic that binds the functions with the core application framework and other third-party libraries.

Using Parameters in the Functions

The previous example function used no parameters. In real-world applications, that's not the case, as programs are often complex and complicated. To take advantage of functions, you must create functions that use parameters and perform tasks.

From the inspiration of the previous example, let us assume that there are two users for our application, and we need to wish them their names.

Program Code:

```
def sample():

        # This function gives a welcome message to the user
        print( "Hello ! Hope you are fine, Sam. Good morning" )
        print( "Hello ! Hope you are fine, Tom. Good morning")
```

sample()

First, you must create two print statements and use both input/ conditionals to verify the user's display of the correct output. This is quite complex and unnecessary as parameters can help you create dynamic welcome messages for your user. Not just for two but thousands of users with just a tiny variation while creating a function.

For example, take this example function with a single parameter that can help you create a dynamic message.

Program Code:

```
def sample(name):
```

"This is an example function with a single parameter."

```
        print ( "Hello "+ name + " Glad that you are back here. Good Morning ")
```

sample('Sam')

sample('Tom')

sample('Rick')

sample('Damon')

Output:

Hello Sam. Glad that you are back here. Good Morning

Hello Tom. Glad that you are back here. Good Morning

Hello Rick. Glad that you are back here. Good Morning

Hello Damon. Glad that you are back here. Good Morning

Explanation:

A function is created with the name 'sample,' and in between parenthesis, the parameter 'name' is defined. You may not need to specify the data type for this parameter because the Python interpreter is intelligent enough to parse any data value the user provides.

The programmer called the parameter in the print function and divided the string using the arithmetic operator. So, whenever the user provides input, it will be placed between the default strings.

The developer has called the function with the parameter input in the following lines. The parameter cannot be defaulted for complex applications but will depend on the user inputs. For this example, we have used the default parameters. Sam, Tom, Rick, and Damon are the parameters that the developer provides.

If you want to create more advanced functions, you can utilize the functionality of arguments provided by Python.

Passing Arguments

All modern applications use parameters for the functions to utilize their complete capabilities. We gave default arguments for the function parameter in the previous example program. However, always providing parameters by default is not ideal for Python developers. All parameters have arguments that users can pass to the function. While there are several ways to pass arguments to the function parameters, positional and keyword arguments are the most popular.

Positional Arguments

With positional arguments, the programmers usually directly provide the values for the function parameters. It may seem confusing, but many programmers often use it because it is easier to implement. With positional arguments, it becomes necessary to remember the order you are passing them.

Program Code:

```python
def football(country,number):

        # This describes how many times a country has won a FIFA world cup
        print ( country + " has won FIFA " + number + "times")

football('Argentina' , 4)

football ('England', 2)
```

Output:

Argentina has won FIFA 4 times

England has won FIFA 2 times

In the above example, the arguments for the first example are 'Argentina' and 4. As data types are not provided, the Python interpreter will automatically determine the value type and pass it to the function.

As there is no definite way for programmers to understand the data type they want to use, parameter names play a significant role. With just a glance, you can understand that a country uses a literal string, whereas a number uses an integer data type. A comma usually separates all the arguments.

As shown below, it is easy to make mistakes while using positional arguments.

Program Code:

```
def football(country,number):

        # This describes how many times a country has won a FIFA world cup
        print ( country + " has won FIFA " + number + "times")

football( 4, 'Argentina')
```

football (2, 'England')

Output:

4 has won FIFA Argentina times

2 has won FIFA England times

While the function provides an output, the above output doesn't make sense because the arguments are provided for opposite parameters.

To solve these minor problems with positional arguments, developers can use Keyword Arguments to define function parameters.

Keyword Arguments

With keyword arguments, you can directly pass arguments to the function parameter. Keyword arguments use parameter = value format to give arguments to any function.

Keyword Arguments cause less confusion but take more time to implement and hence are not often used by developers working on complex projects that involve a lot of code.

Program Code:

```
def football(country,number):

        # This describes how many times a country has won a FIFA world cup
        print ( country + " has won FIFA " + number + "times")

football( country = 'Argentina' , number = 4)
```

football (country = 'England', number = 2)

Output:

Argentina has won FIFA 4 times

England has won FIFA 2 times

Here, parameter = argument is the format by which keyword arguments have been defined. For example, in-country = 'Argentina,' country is the parameter, whereas 'Argentina' is the given argument.

Understanding Modules

A group of meaningful functions usually form modules in a programming language. Whenever you want to use these groups of functions in any software component, you can just import the module and call the function with your arguments for the parameters.

Importing modules in Python is much better than the traditional languages such as C and C+. Many programmers import modules to use methods in the module and add additional capabilities on top of it.

Syntax:

        import { Name of the module }

Example:

import clock

The above syntax will import all the inbuilt functions present in the clock module to your program; hence, you can now provide your own arguments to these methods.

What Does Import Do?

Import is an inbuilt Python library function that copies all the functions in a specific file and links it to your current file. It gives you permission to use methods that don't belong to the present file. Creating modules will help you stop writing the same code repeatedly.

How to Create Modules?

While importing modules from third-party libraries and frameworks saves you time, you must be aware of creating modules on your own as a developer.

Let us suppose you are making a web application for a torrent service. You now need to write a lot of functions to make the application work. For better organization, you can create a networking module and enter all the functions related to networking in this module. Next, you can create a module associated with GUI and several functions to help you create a good-looking application.

How to Create?

To create a Python module, you first need to create a text file with a .py extension.

Once the .py file is created, you can now enter all the functions in this file.

For example, you can add the below function used to multiply two numbers in the .py module we have created just now.

File – samplemodule.py

```
def product(x,y):

        # This can be used to create a product between two numbers
        z = x * y
        return z
        # The product will be printed as the output
```

As the module is created, we will show a sample program that imports the above function.

Program Code:

import samplemodule

Click the enter button, and now all the functions in that particular module will be accessible for a Python programmer working on other projects.

Program Code:

samplemodule.product(3,6)

Output:

18

The program will automatically detect the product function, and depending on the arguments provided, the product will be displayed on the computer screen.

Built—In Functions and Modules

Developers can utilize several built-in functions and modules while creating complex and complicated software applications. While user-built functions are tremendous and provide freedom to solve complex problems, they are still hard to implement and sometimes unnecessary because built-in functions can do the work for you.

1. print()

This is probably the most popular built-in function in the Python library. From beginners to experienced programmers, everyone use print() statement to send output to the computer screen. Usually, the content you want to display on the screen should be placed between the quotes.

Program Code:

Print ("This is an example ")

Output:

This is an example

2. abs()

This built-in function provides absolute value for any integer data type. Most of the time, if negative integers are provided, this function will make them whole.

Program Code:

```
x = -24
```

print (abs(x))

Output:

24

3. round ()

Round () is an inbuilt mathematical function that provides the closest integer number for any provided floating-point numbers.

Program Code:

```
x = 2.46
y = 3.12
print(round(x))
```

print(round(y))

Output:

2

3

4. max()

max() is a built-in Python function that can be used to output the maximum number between a group of numbers. You can use this function for any data type, such as lists or variables.

Program Code:

A= 45

B = 43

C = 23

Solution = max(A,B,C)

print(Solution)

Output:

45

5. min()

min() is a Python built-in function that can be used to output the minimum number between a group of numbers.

Program Code:

A= 45

B = 43

C = 23

Solution = min(A,B,C)

print(Solution)

Output:

23

6. sorted()

Sorted () is a built-in Python function that can sort out all the elements in a list using an ascending or descending order according to your choice.

Program Code:

88

x = (2,323,21,5,242,11)

y = sorted(x)

print(y)

Output:

[2, 5, 11, 21, 242, 323]

7. sum()

Sum () is a particular built-in function that will add all the elements present in a tuple. Make sure that before using this in-built function, all the elements in the tuple are of the same data type. If not, the program will end with a type error, as adding values related to two different data types is impossible.

Program Code:

x = (32,43,11,12,19)

y = sum(x)

print(y)

Output:

117

8. len()

len() is a built-in function that provides information about the number of elements in a list or tuple.

Program Code:

x= (1,23,32,11,12)

y = len(x)

print(y)

Output:

5

9. type()

Type () built-in function will provide information about the list of variables using data type. If it is a function, then the details about parameters and arguments will also be displayed.

Program Code:

```
X = 23.2121
print(type(x))
```

Output:

<class 'float'>

String Methods

Strings are popular data types and hence need more attention than other data types from the programmer. Python core library provides tens of different built-in functions to help programmers make the most out of the data stored using string data types.

1. strip()

strip() is a built-in string function that deletes the arguments provided as a parameter for the function. All the instances where the arguments are present will be stripped.

Program Code:

```
x = "Welcome"
print( x.strip('me'))
```

Output:

Welco

2. replace()

Replace () is a built-in python function where a part of the string will replace with another. If there are many words in the same string data type, you can provide how many words you want to replace as a parameter.

Program Code:

example = "This is not a good sign"

print(example.replace('good' , 'bad'))

Output:

This is not a bad sign

3. split()

Split (), an in-built python function, will automatically split a string when the arguments you have provided first appear in the text.

Program Code:

example = "There are nine planets"

print(example.split('re')

Output:

['The', ' a', ' nine planets']

As the argument we have provided is repeated two times, the string is split into three parts.

4. join()

join() is a special Python function that lets you add a separator between the elements in a list.

Program Code:

x= [23,11,12,56]

sample ="~"

sample = sample.join(x)

Output:

23 ~ 11 ~ 12 ~ 56

Exercises

Create a Python program to generate ten numbers randomly that automatically finds the maximum value in those ten numbers. Use the max() method to solve this problem.

Create a list, reverse all the elements, and add them.

Write a Python program to input ten strings and reverse each one.

Write a recursive function to find the factorial of 100

Create a 3-page essay using string manipulation techniques. Represent all of them just like how you represent them on paper. Use as many methods as you can.

Write a Python program that provides rows related to Pascal's triangle.

Create a Python program that automatically extracts an article from Wikipedia according to the input.

Create a Python program to create a color scheme for all the RGB colors.

Chapter 10: Object Oriented Programming (OOP)

What Is Object-Oriented Programming?

OOP is a popular programming paradigm where classes and objects are used to group functions defined in a program into logical templates.

A class consists of a group of data members or methods that can easily be accessed using a dot notation. Due to object behavior, classes are accessible to variables and methods outside the class.

Real-World Example:

Let us assume that you are creating an application that explains details about different vehicles and different models of those vehicles.

With object-oriented programming, a developer usually creates a function for each vehicle and then again for each model. It may seem easy if there are only a few vehicle models, but code reuse becomes hectic for developers with the increase in vehicle models.

On the other hand, with Object-oriented programming, the programmer will first create a 'vehicle' class and define various properties and values. Next, the developer will take a separate category for each vehicle type. Instead of creating functions for each property again, the application developer can access and call all those properties with just a simple dot notation due to the Object-oriented programming paradigm.

Object-oriented programming saves a lot of time and makes it easy for Python developers to reuse their code with the help of features such as Polymorphism and inheritance.

How to Create and Use a Class

Python provides a simple syntax rule to create classes in Python.

Class ClassName :

Example:

Class Cat:

Here, "Cat" is the class name. Remember that you cannot use reserved keywords for class names. Let us now create a simple example about cats using Python classes.

Example:

Class Cat():

" This is used to model a Cat."

Def __init__(self, breed, age) :

""" Initialize breed and age attributes """

self.breed = breed

self.age = age

Def meow(self) :

""" This describes a cat meowing """

print(self.breed.title() + " cats meow loudly")

Def purr(self)

""" This describes a cat purring """

print(self.breed.title() + " cats purrs loudly")

Explanation

Firstly, we have created a class with the name Cat. There are no attributes or parameters in the parentheses of the class because this is a new class where we are starting everything from scratch. Advanced classes may have many parameters and attribute to solve complex problems required for real-world applications.

Immediately after the class name, a docstring called ' This is used to model a cat' describes the necessity for this class. It would be best to practice writing docstrings more often to help other programmers understand the details about your class.

In the next step, we created an _init_ () method and defined three arguments. Python runs this unique function automatically when an object instance is made from a class. _init_ function is a mandatory Python function; without it, the interpreter will reject the object initiation.

Similarly, we have created two other functions, 'meow' and 'purr', with arguments for each. In this example, these two functions print a statement. In real-world scenarios, methods will perform higher-level functionalities.

You should have observed the 'self' argument in all three methods in the above class. Self is an automatic function argument that needs to be entered for every method in a class.

All the variables can be called in a class using a dot operator (.). For example, 'self.age' is an example of calling a variable using a dot operator.

Exercises:

Write a Python program to import all the essential classes in Pandas machine learning library.

Use a built-in Python module to list all the built-in functions that Python supports. Create a Python program to list all these functions in a table format.

Using object-oriented programming, create an OOP model for a library management system. Introduce all the modules that can be used and list all the arguments that need to be given.

Write a Python class of shapes to calculate the area of any figure.

Write a class and create both global and instance class variables.

Use Python classes to convert Roman numerical standards to the decimal system.

How to Create Objects

An object in Python programming is an entity that has a state and behavior associated with it. Everything that is inside a class can be treated as an object. For example, a variable created inside a class can be used as an object. Programmers often always use objects but are unaware of them.

What does an object consist of?

All the objects consist of a state. A state usually reflects the properties associated with an object.

All the objects have a behavior. An object's behavior changes according to the method it is being used in.

All objects have an identity. Identity helps objects to interact with other objects.

For example, let us assume that there is a dog class describing different dog breeds and their behavior. In that class, objects can be of various kinds.

The name of the dog is usually the identity of the object.

Attributes such as dog breed, age, and color can be described as the state of an object.

Behavior such as barking, sleeping, or running related to a dog can be called behaviors of an object.

How to create an object

To create an object, all you have to do is initiate it using a name. For example, if the 'Dog' class has been defined, we can write:

Program Code:

obj = Dog()

This will create an object called 'obj' belonging to the Dog class.

Understanding the Self Method

Python programmers need to be aware of the self-method, which is created automatically when a class is created.

A self-method is quite similar to the concept of pointers used in other high-level programming languages such as C and C++.

What should we be aware of?

Make sure you give at least one argument with the self-method if you want to call the methods.

Every method called by an object will be automatically converted to a self-object.

Understanding __init__ Method

__init__ method is similar to constructors in C++ and Java. Whenever a class is initiated, it will run as a default method. So, as a developer, if you want to create an object with an initial value, you need to enter those values to __init__method.

We will now create a Python program using self, and the ____init__ method.

Program Code:

```
Class Geography:
    # Create a class attribute now
    attr1 = "country"
    # Create an instance attribute
    def __init__(self,name):
        self.name = name
# Now create an object and instantiate it
USA = Geography("USA")
UK= Geography("UK")
# Accessing Class Attributes
print ( "USA is a {} " .format(USA.attr1))
print( "UK is a {} " .format(UK.attr1))
# Accessing instance attributes
```

print("Country name is {}" .format(USA.name))

print("Country name is {}" .format(UK.name))

   Output:

The USA is a country

The UK is a country

The country's name is the USA

The country's name is the UK

In the above example, we created a class and class and instance attributes. You don't need to do this every time while creating a class, and we just provide a program for you to understand how classes and objects work right from the time they are initiated.

A class name should be provided.

At least one attribute should be created.

A self-argument should be provided along with an ___init___ method.

Start object instantiation.

After object instantiation, you can create class, and instance attributes that can utilize the object created.

How to Create Classes and Objects With Methods?

We will now create a usual program code that developers follow to develop methods and call them using objects.

   Program Code:

```
class Geography:

    # Create a class attribute

    attr1 = "country"
```

```python
# Create an instance attribute
def __init__(self,countryname):
    self.countryname = countryname
def governance(self):
    print("This country is {}" .format(self.countryname))
# Object instantiation
USA = Geography( "USA")
UK = Geography("UK")
USA.governance()
UK.governance()
```

Output:

This country is USA

This country is UK

Explanation:

In the above example, a class attribute is created, and then a method is created along with the __init__ function. In the end, the object is instantiated, and the object is accessed by using dot notation.

Inheritance

Inheritance is one of the essential features of Object-Oriented programming. Inheritance refers to defining a new class without adding new methods or arguments but deriving them from other classes. The new class is usually known as the child class, whereas the class from which all the methods are inherited is called the parent class.

Real-World Example:

Inheritance becomes handy in many situations while creating real-world applications. For example, assume that you are making a camera mobile application for the iOS platform.

While developing the application, you may have to create several modules for several functions the application offers. In a few months of development, you have observed that you are reusing the code for GUI interfaces as your team is still following function-oriented programming.

To save time and money, you decided to implement an Object-oriented paradigm for your project. As you are now using the OOP paradigm, you can derive the code already written for GUI interfaces and interlink them to the new classes you are writing. This reduces time and energy and allows programmers to add new features without rewriting the old ones.

The syntax for Python inheritance:

```
class BaseClass:
    { Body of base class }
class DerivedClass(Baseclass):
    { Body of derived class }
```

Note:
Both base and derived classes should still follow all the class rules described before.

Program Code:

```
# Defining the class 'polygon'

class polygon:

    def __init__(self,sides):

        self.sides = sides

    def dispsides(self):

        for i in range(self.sides):

            print("side", i+1 )
```

```
# Defining the class 'square' starting from the previous one

class square(polygon):

    def __init__(self):

        self.sides = int(input( "Side of the square:"))

    def findArea(self):

        a = self.sides

        # Calculate the area

        s = a*a

        print ( "The area of the square is," s)

# Defining a polygon with five sides

x = polygon(5)

x.dispsides()

# Defining a square, asking the user the length of the edge and computing its area

x2 = square()
```

x2.findArea()

Explanation:

We first defined the class 'polygon' in the above program and created an object (polygon) with five sides. It is possible to display the sides thanks to 'dispsides.'

Then the class 'square' is derived. In this case, the user must specify the side of the square's edge as soon as an object from this class is created.

When the method 'findArea' is called by the object, it will use the user's input and output the area of the square for the user.

In the future, you can create another polygon class by just creating a method to calculate the area.

Output:

side 1

side 2

side 3

side 4

side 5

Side of the square:15

The area of the square is 225

With enough information about Object-Oriented Programming, you will now be able to create classes and objects that can interact with each other to develop software that utilizes many components and performs several tasks. To learn more about Object-oriented programming, try looking at the open-source code hosted on Github.

Chapter 11: Files in Python

Files and File Paths

Python programmers usually work with different files using two parameters. The first one is the file name which helps people find it easily, whereas the file path describes where it was.

For example, if example.pdf is the name of a file, then " C:/ users/ downloads/example.pdf" is the path format of a file. The file name 'example.pdf,' pdf is the file's extension.

To handle files, operating systems usually use an effective file management system.

Note:

To be aware of different file management techniques, it is essential to know the basics of file managers used in other operating systems.

For example, Windows users use file explorer, whereas Mac systems use Finder to manage files. Irrespective of the operating system and file manager you are using, files are usually placed in a logical hierarchical manner with the help of root directories, folders, and subdirectories.

Understanding Hierarchical Arrangement of Files

All Python programmers need to enter the whole path of the file location for the program to detect the file location. The entire path of the file is usually written hierarchically so that the directory, subdirectories, and folders are determined from the path.

For example, in ' C://users/sample / example.pdf,' C is the system's root directory, and both samples and users can be called the subdirectories in this root directory.

As there can be different files with the same name in other directories, it is essential to use the whole path to recognize the file's location.

Note:

As a python programmer, you need to know that Windows file systems use Backslashes to distinguish between the root directory and sub directions. In contrast, other operating systems, such as Mac and Linux, use forward slashes to differentiate between root directories and subdirectories.

If you are not interested in using back or forward slashes for whatever reason while entering code on the terminal, you can use a particular function known as os.path.join.

Program Code:

os.path.join('D', 'first', 'second')

Output:

'D\first\second'

Knowing Current Working Directory

As a Python programmer, while running complex code, you often need to interact with different files in the same directory. To help programmers easily interact with other files in the same directory, a function known as os.getcwd() can be used. Once your absolute path is detected, all the files in the directory or subdirectory will be displayed as an output.

Example:

os.getcwd()

' D: \ linux \ samplefiles \ python '

The absolute path of your current directory location is displayed in the output. You can now use operating system commands such as cd to list the files in the directory.

Creating New Folders

Several Python software often requires users to create files or the application to create files independently in different directories. For example, a save file for a game is automatically generated by the software without the interference of a user.

Several Python software often needs users to create files or requires the application to create files independently in different directories. For example, a save file for a game is automatically generated by the software without the interference of a user. All python programmers need to be aware of creating new folders for the applications they build.

Python provides a function called os.makedirs() to create a new directory.

Program Code:

import os

os.makedirs(' D: /user1/ python/sample')

In the above example, we have first imported the module where the above system function design is present. In the next step, we have called the makedirs() function with a path as the function parameter. Sample is the new folder we created in the python directory using the above function. You can verify by opening your file manager or using the cd button on a command prompt.

Note:

Ensure that you provide an absolute path for the directory where you want to create a new folder.

File Management Functions

Files are complex and need a lot of inbuilt functions to help them function better. As a Python programmer, you can easily manipulate, open or close files from your IDE or terminal. Python interpreter can run both .txt and .py extension files by default.

If you want to open or manipulate file types such as pdf and jpg, you need to install third-party libraries capable of doing this. These file types are known as binary file types by experienced Python programmers.

Initially, to help you quickly understand the concepts of Files, we will first create a file called example.txt on the path "D: /users/python/example.txt." Feel free to use your path for creating a file.

We will use this example txt file to describe file functions such as open(), close(), Write() and read().

Let us assume that the example.txt has content, as shown below.

Content:
This is a Python file manipulation sample sheet.
How to Open Files With the open() Function?

Opening files using a Python command is pretty straightforward. All you have to know is the absolute path of the file and the usage of the open() function.

Program Code:

```
filemanagement = open ( ' D: /users / python / example.txt ')
```

This function will open the file on your terminal or IDE

The above example uses the open() function along with the parameter. In the example, the parameter is the path provided to open a file. When a file is opened, the Python interpreter will not be able to read or write to the file, but the user can read the file using the default viewer in which the file was opened.

Ensure that you have software installed to open the files before executing this statement. If you try to open a video file with the format .mp4, but if there is no native software that can open this file, it will not be a feasible solution.

What Happens?

When the interpreter finds the open() function, it creates a new file object, and all the changes performed during this phase should be saved to reflect on the original file. The Python interpreter will ignore all the changes if the file is not saved.

How to Read Files With the read() Function?

Once Python opens a file using the open() function, it creates a new object, and hence now, it becomes easy for the Python interpreter to use the read() function to read the entire file's content.

Program Code:

reading = filemanagement.read()

#This read() function will scan all the content present in the file

reading

Output:

This is a Python file manipulation sample sheet.

In the above example, we have used the read() function and have sent all the scanned data from the file to a new variable known as 'reading.' You can also send the information into files to lists, tuples, or dictionaries, depending on the complexity of the file you are dealing with.

While the above read() function has just printed the content in the file, you can use the readlines() function to organize the content in a file to new lines.

We will provide a simple example to understand this special feature in Python.

First, create a new file name in your working directory called 'newfile.txt.'

Once the file is opened, enter a few lines of any information, as shown below.

newfile.txt:

This is a sample document.

We are just creating lines.

We will use this data to manipulate text.

Python interpreter is efficient.

enough to make this possible

Now call the readlines() functions on the terminal.

Program Code:

adv = open(readlines.txt)

This variable helps us open a new file with the name provided

adv. readlines()

Output:

[' This is a sample document \n,' ' We are just creating lines \n, ' We will use this data to manipulate text,' ' Python interpreter is efficient,' ' enough to make this possible']

The output has presented all the lines in the file with a newline character \n. There are a lot of advanced file functions like this that you can use while creating real-world applications.

How to Write Content to Files With the write() Function?

As a Python programmer, you can also enter new data into any file using the write() function. The write() function is quite similar to the print() function that programmers use to display content on the screen. The write () function displays the content of your favorable file name.

Programmers can open the file using write mode with the help of the open() function. All you have to do is append an argument for the interpreter to understand that you want to open your file and add your own content.

Once you complete writing content into the file, you can use the close() method to close the file and be automatically saved in its default location.

Program Code:

example = open('filemanagement.txt', 'w')

#This makes the file open in write mode

example.write (' This is how you need to open write mode \n ')

The output will display the content on the screen and provide the number of characters on the screen.

You can also use 'a' to append text as an argument.

For Example:

example = open ('filemanagement.txt', 'a')

The file first opens in write mode

example.write('This is a new version')

The above statement will be added to the file provided

example.close()

To verify whether or not the text has been appended, you can use the read function as shown below.

example = open(example.txt)

sample = read(example.txt)

print(sample)

Output:

This is a new version

Copying files and folders

Usually, you can easily copy, paste or cut files and folders using the default file manager functionalities such as Windows Explorer and Mac finder. However, developers creating Python software need to use a built-in library known as shutil to create programming components that can be used to copy, move, or delete files quickly.

To use the default functions present in the shutil library, you must first import them.

Syntax:
> import shutil

Copying Files or Folders

To copy files or folders from one location to another, you can simply use shutil.copy() function. This function usually has two parameters: the source of the file and the second parameter being the destination of the file.

Example:

shutil.copy (' C: \ user1 \ python \ sample.txt' , C: \ user2\ python')

In the above example, a file named sample.txt present in the Python folder of the user1 directory is copied to the python folder in the user2 directory.

If you want to copy the file to a new file according to your choice, then you may need to define the file name in the second parameter, as shown below.

Example:

shutil.copy (' C: \ user1 \ python \ sample.txt' , C: \ user2\ python\ sample1.txt')

All the file contents in the sample.txt file will be copied and added to the sample1.txt file.

Moving and Renaming Files and Folders

Moving a file or folder takes less time but is considered a bit risky compared to copying files as you will not have a backup copy. When you move your files, they will be deleted entirely from the current directory and transferred to the new directory you provided.

Python programmers can use shutil.move() function to quickly move files from one location to another.

Program Code:

shutil.move (' C: \ user1 \ python \ sample.txt' , C: \ user2\ python')

The above example will move the file 'sample1.text' to another directory.

If you are worried about having a file with the same name in the directory you are trying to save, you can use the syntax below.

Program Code:

shutil.move (' C: \ user1 \ python \ sample.txt' , C: \ user2\ python.txt')

The above example can also be called a simple renaming of the moved file.

Deleting Files and Folders

Python also provides three different functions for the developers to delete files according to their convenience.

os.unlink(path) – This function will delete only the file that was provided in the path

Example:

os.unlink(' C "\ user1\ python1\ arithmetic.text')

The file named arithmetic.txt will be deleted permanently.

os.rmdir(path)

This function will delete a whole folder that is provided as the parameter.

Example:

os.rmdir(' C " \ user1\ python')

The folder named 'python' will be permanently deleted.

shutil.rmtree (path)

This function will first recognize the tree path and will delete all the folders and files that are present in this tree path.

Example:

shutil.rmtree(' C: \ user1 ')

All the files and folders present in the user1 directory will be deleted.

Chapter 12: Exception Handling

'Try' and 'Except' Statements

Try and except are the leading programming components developers must be aware of while creating exception handling tasks. The try block is where the developers need to mention the chances of finding the error in the Python interpreter. On the other hand, the except block needs information about what to do if a specific error we defined occurs during program execution.

Program Code:

```
# Let's write a try and except block in a function
def divide64(number):
    try:
        x = 64/number
        print(x)
    except ZeroDivisionError:
        print ( "Cannot divide by 0")


divide64(2)
divide64(0)
divide64(64)
```

Output:

32.0

Cannot divide by 0

1.0

What Happened?

We first defined a try and except block that explained to the interpreter where we can expect an error popup and provided what information should be displayed if there is an error.

Chapter 13: Elements of Advanced Programming

GitHub for Programmers

GitHub is important for programmers as it makes it easy to work remotely with teams. GitHub depends on a GIT repository that is peer-to-peer based, and hence your code changes will be reflected in your teammates' computers as soon as they connect to the internet.

GitHub offers two versions - free and professional versions. When you use the free version of GitHub, all your code will be available to everyone who can access Github. However, with a professional version, your code will be private, and only your team members can access the code. All private repositories use high encryption algorithms to protect your data.

Why Is Github Essential for Python Programmers?

Irrespective of your computer domain, you may have to use third-party libraries and frameworks in Github while creating projects. You can either use GitHub or several third-party clients that will help you to interact with the local repositories instantly.

GitHub and all Git-supported clients use dependencies to sync libraries and modules into your code easily. You can change the code using the 'commit' option the Git server uses.

To create a new repository in your GIT server, use the below command on your Python shell.

Python Command:

$ git config —global root "sample project."

Once the git code is entered on the console, a new project will be created, and now you can create directories for your project. Use the below command to create a directory on your project's root.

$mkdir. ("Enter the name of the repository")

If you are unaware of the information about the GIT server or project you are dealing with, you can enter the below command on your console.

$ git status

With these prerequisites, you are ready to start creating your open-source project to help fellow programmers in your domain.

Pip Package Manager

All operating systems provide applications for their users. Python is not an operating system but just an interpreter that can run software using Python. Any software not written in Python cannot be run using a Python interpreter because it is not capable of understanding the source code used by that software.

There are several thousands of free and paid Python software to download from different sources. A simple google search can fetch thousands of results about Python software for your domain. You, however, need at least a little knowledge about executable files if you want to install this software on your own.

To help programmers find their required software easily, Python provides package managers that developers can use to download package files into their operating system and immediately execute with the help of these managers. While there are many third-party package managers for Python, the default pip is the most popular one that every Python programmer needs to know.

What Can You Do With Pip?

You can install new packages and dependencies.

You can find an index to list all the Python package repositories available in pip servers.

Use it to review the requirements before installing the software.

Use it to uninstall any packages and dependencies that you no longer need.

First, check whether or not pip is installed in your system. Typically, pip is included along with the Python package.

Terminal Code:

$ pip —version

The package manager is installed on your system if it prints out the pip version information details. If not, you may need to download it from the official website and install it manually.

How to Install Packages?

You must always use the same syntax format shown below to install packages.

$ pip install software name

For example, if you want to install a package called "Tensorflow" into your system. Then you may need to use the below syntax.

$ pip install tensor flow

Before installing, if you want to check the metadata related to the content, then use the below command.

$ pip show tensorflow

The output of this terminal code will be about a lot of metadata information such as the Author, Package name, and location of the package.

To uninstall any packages installed on your system using the pip package manager, use the below code syntax format.

Syntax:

$ pip uninstall nameofthepackage

For example, if you want to uninstall the tensor flow package you have installed before, use the below command.

$ pip uninstall tensorflow

You can also search packages using the below code format.

$ pip search packagename

This will display all the packages from the package index for you to analyze and choose from.

Virtual Environment

Usually, when programmers install packages, they install several dependencies. Sometimes these dependencies may coincide with other software, and these packages may not install. To help developers create independent projects, an isolated virtual environment can be created using the 'virtualenv' package.

First, you must install this 'virtualenv' package using the pip package manager.

Terminal Command:

$ pip install virtualenv

Once the package is installed, you can use the below command to create a new directory using a virtual machine.

$ virtualenv sample

All the files, software, and packages you install in the terminal command will be saved into this new directory without messing up with any in-built dependencies or packages in your system.

You need first to activate the virtual machine using the below command.

Terminal Command:

$ source sample/bin/activate

When all your packages are installed, you can simply deactivate this virtual environment using the below command.

Terminal Command:

(sample) $ deactivate

Understanding sys Module

As a Python programmer, you need to be completely aware of how a Python interpreter functions. An interpreter usually parses every variable, literal, or method present in the code and will execute a logically written program while checking for syntax, type, and index errors. As a developer, it is common for you to check how an interpreter functions and stores sensitive information required for using specific software.

Python makes it easy for developers to check this information with the help of the Sys module.

import sys

You can derive all the methods present in the 'sys' library using this command.

path

This argument from the sys library will help you know about the Python interpreter's default path installed in your system.

print(sys.path)

Argv

This method will list out all the existing modules that are present in the system.

print(sys.Argv)

copyright

This method will display the copyright details of the Python interpreter or software to the user.

119

print(sys.copyright)

getrefcount

   This method will display how often a program uses a variable or object.

print(sys.getrefcount(variable))

Conclusion

I appreciate you reading this book. People are becoming increasingly hooked on the modern comforts of smart technology, and this trend will continue for a very long time. You are now prepared to develop your original, innovative tech ideas, transform them into a significant tech startup firm, and lead humanity toward a brighter future, thanks to all the guidelines in this book.

The thing about computer programming is that your learning will never stop. Even if you think you have the basics down pat, you don't use what you have learned regularly. Computer programming is changing almost daily, and it's up to you to keep up with everything going on. To that end, you would be well advised to join a few Python communities. This will let you know about the latest and allow you to describe your own experiences. You'll be able to offer advice and assistance and get help from others when needed.

Eventually, you will be in a position to be able to help the newbies on the scene, and it is then that you will realize just how far you have come.

Python is a functional programming language with a wide range of applications. It is practical, effective, and straightforward to use. It will be a valuable resource and point of reference for you as a programmer in the future. You can make anything you can imagine. Don't be tentative about giving something new a try.

Keep in mind that knowledge is useless if it is not used. The time you spend reading this book to learn programming without actual programming will be wasted.

The goal of this book is to explain Python to beginning programmers. With this book, you should write basic and even more complex programs with multiple objects.

Becoming a Pythonista will require plenty of practice. Also, feel free to devise your exercises and practice. Good luck and happy programming!